Campbell's®

4 Ingredients or Less

Four Ingredients or Less

Publications
International Ltd.

Favorite Brand Name Recipes at www.fbnr.com

Vice President, Campbell's Kitchen
Lucinda Ayers
Group Manager, Campbell's Kitchen
Catherine Marschean-Spivak
Manager, Campbell's Kitchen
Jane Freiman
Assistant Manager
Donna Liotto-Scocozza
Product Specialist
Erin Garvey

Pictured on the front cover: 2-Step Chicken 'n' Biscuits (page 42).

Pictured on the back cover (clockwise from top): Chocolate and Coconut Cream Fondue (page 9), Easy Beef & Pasta (page 62), Game-Winning Drumsticks (page 38), and Grilled Beef Steak with Sauteed Onions (page 54).

ISBN-13: 978-1-4127-2477-7
ISBN-10: 1-4127-2477-5

Manufactured in China.

8 7 6 5 4 3 2 1

Microwave Cooking: Microwave ovens vary in wattage. Use the cooking times as guidelines and check for doneness before adding more time.

Preparation/Cooking Times: Preparation times are based on the approximate amount of time required to assemble the recipe before cooking, baking, chilling, or serving. These times include preparation steps such as measuring, chopping, and mixing. The fact that some preparation and cooking can be done simultaneously is taken into account. Preparation of optional ingredients and serving suggestions is not included.

Contents

21

26

50

Note: In recipes with 5 ingredients, the extra ingredient is water.

There's more time to enjoy family and friends
when you simplify food preparation

Less Is More

Life today runs at a pretty fast pace for all of us, and you're not alone if it seems like you have more to do and less time to do it. One of the places we really feel the crunch is in the kitchen. It's always a challenge to create well-balanced meals while balancing busy schedules, too.

When food preparation time is short, you need recipes that are long on simplicity: familiar techniques, easy steps, few ingredients, and a lot less fuss. Campbell's® has come to the rescue with this collection of fast and tasty dishes made with just four ingredients or fewer. These recipes couldn't be quicker or more simple—and you probably already have many of the ingredients on hand right now in your pantry!

Best of all, this collection includes delicious and delightfully easy ideas for almost any occasion, whether you're preparing for a party, trying to feed a gang of hungry kids, or just putting out a simple weeknight supper. Every recipe is designed to help you spend less time in the kitchen and more time doing what you really enjoy: connecting with your family and friends.

Chocolate and Coconut Cream Fondue
Recipe on page 12

Party Starters

It only takes three ingredients to create a party: a place to gather, the pleasure of good company, and food that's festive and fun. But if you add just one more ingredient, you can make your event more than just a great get-together—you can make it an occasion that everyone will remember and enjoy, including the cook! That magic ingredient is simplicity.

This collection features entertaining favorites that never fail to get the party started—appetizers, finger foods, fun-to-share fondues, delicious dips, and celebration beverages—all made with just 4 ingredients or fewer so pre-party preparation is quick and simple.

Honey Mustard Chicken Bites

Prep Time: 15 minutes
Bake Time: 15 minutes

1½ pounds skinless, boneless chicken breasts, cut into 1-inch pieces

1 jar (12 ounces) refrigerated honey mustard salad dressing

2 cups Pepperidge Farm® Herb Seasoned Stuffing, crushed

2 tablespoons orange juice

DIP chicken into ¾ **cup** dressing. Coat with stuffing.

PLACE chicken on baking sheet. Bake at 400°F. for 15 minutes or until chicken is no longer pink.

MIX remaining dressing and orange juice in medium saucepan over medium heat. Heat through. Serve with chicken for dipping.

Makes about 40 appetizers.

TIP:
To microwave dip, mix remaining dressing and orange juice in microwavable bowl. Microwave on **HIGH** 1 minute or until hot.

Italiano Fondue

Prep Time: 5 minutes
Cook Time: 10 minutes

1¾ cups Prego® Traditional Pasta Sauce

¼ cup dry red wine

1 cup shredded mozzarella cheese (4 ounces)

Suggested Dippers: Warm Pepperidge Farm® Garlic Bread, cut into cubes, meatballs, sliced cooked Italian pork sausage, breaded mozzarella sticks, whole mushrooms

MIX pasta sauce and wine in medium saucepan over medium heat for 5 minutes for alcohol to evaporate.

POUR into fondue pot. Add cheese. Let stand for 5 minutes for cheese to melt slightly. Serve warm with dippers.

Makes 2 cups.

Italiano Fondue

Chocolate and Coconut Cream Fondue

Prep Time: 5 minutes
Cook Time: 10 minutes

1 can (15 ounces) cream of coconut

2 tablespoons rum (optional) **or** 1 teaspoon rum extract

1 package (12 ounces) semi-sweet chocolate pieces

Suggested Dippers: Assorted Pepperidge Farm® Cookies, Pepperidge Farm® Graham Giant Goldfish® Baked Snack Crackers, whole strawberries, banana chunks, dried **or** fresh pineapple chunks

MIX cream of coconut, rum and chocolate in medium saucepan over medium heat. Heat through until chocolate is melted, stirring occasionally.

POUR into fondue pot. Serve warm with dippers.

Makes 3 cups.

Quick Cheesy Fondue

Prep Time: 5 minutes
Cook Time: 10 minutes

1 can (10½ ounces) Campbell's® Condensed French Onion Soup

¼ cup dry sherry

1 package (8 ounces) cream cheese, softened

1 cup shredded Gruyère cheese (4 ounces)

Suggested Dippers: French bread cubes, warm Pepperidge Farm® Garlic Bread, cut into cubes, cooked meatballs, cubes of deli roast beef, steamed baby red potatoes

MIX soup and sherry in medium saucepan over medium heat for 5 minutes for alcohol to evaporate. Add cream cheese. Heat through, stirring occasionally. Add Gruyère cheese. Cook until cheeses are melted.

POUR into a fondue pot. Serve warm with dippers.

Makes 2½ cups.

TIP:
To soften cream cheese, remove from wrapper. On microwavable plate, microwave on **HIGH** 15 seconds.

Quick Cheesy Fondue

Warm French Onion Dip with Crusty Bread

Prep Time: 5 minutes
Bake Time: 30 minutes

1 can (10½ ounces) Campbell's® Condensed French Onion Soup

1 package (8 ounces) cream cheese, softened

1 cup shredded mozzarella cheese (4 ounces)

Bread cubes, crackers **or** vegetables

MIX soup and cream cheese until smooth. Stir in mozzarella cheese. Spread in 1-quart shallow baking dish.

BAKE at 375°F. for 30 minutes or until hot.

SERVE with bread, crackers or vegetables for dipping.

Makes 2 cups.

Fiesta Cilantro Fondue

Prep Time: 5 minutes
Cook Time: 10 minutes

1 can (10¾ ounces) Campbell's® Condensed Creamy Chicken Verde Soup

¼ cup beer

½ cup Pace® Cilantro Salsa

2 cups shredded Cheddar cheese (8 ounces)

Suggested Dippers: French bread cubes, assorted Pepperidge Farm® Crackers, cooked breaded chicken nuggets, steamed vegetables (asparagus spears, broccoli flowerets, red potato wedges), tortilla chips

MIX soup and beer in medium saucepan over medium heat until hot. Add salsa and cheese. Heat through until cheese is melted, stirring occasionally.

POUR into fondue pot. Serve warm with dippers.

Makes 2 cups.

Fiesta Cilantro Fondue

Colossal Queso Dip

Colossal Queso Dip

Prep/Cook Time: 5 minutes

1 can (10¾ ounces) Campbell's®
   Condensed Cheddar Cheese
   Soup

½ cup Pace® Chunky Salsa

1 box (11.5 ounces) Pepperidge
   Farm® Giant Goldfish®
   Crackers

MIX soup and salsa in 1-quart
microwavable casserole. Microwave
on **HIGH** 2½ minutes or until hot,
stirring once.

SERVE with crackers for dipping.

Makes 1½ cups.

Bloody Mary Mocktail

Prep Time: 5 minutes

3 cups V8® 100% Vegetable Juice

1 teaspoon prepared horseradish

1 teaspoon Worcestershire sauce

½ teaspoon hot pepper sauce

   Ice cubes

MIX vegetable juice, horseradish,
Worcestershire and hot pepper sauce.

SERVE over ice.

Makes 3 cups.

Pesto Elephant Ears

Thaw Time: 30 minutes
Prep Time: 20 minutes
Bake Time: 12 minutes

1 package (17.3 ounces) Pepperidge Farm® Frozen Puff Pastry Sheets (2 sheets)

1 egg

1 tablespoon water

3 tablespoons prepared pesto sauce

THAW pastry sheets at room temperature 30 minutes. Preheat oven to 400°F. Mix egg and water.

UNFOLD **1** pastry sheet on lightly floured surface. Spread **half** the pesto evenly on pastry. Starting at short sides, fold pastry toward center, leaving ¼-inch space in center. Fold one side over the other, making a 4-layer rectangle. Repeat with remaining pastry sheet and pesto.

CUT each rectangle into 12 (¾-inch) slices. Place slices cut-side down 2 inches apart on 2 baking sheets. Brush with egg mixture.

BAKE 12 minutes or until golden. Serve warm.

Makes 24 appetizers.

TIP:

To reheat pastries, preheat oven to 400°F. Place pastries on baking sheet. Bake for 2 minutes or until hot.

Napoleons California Style

Thaw Time: 30 minutes
Bake Time: 15 minutes
Prep Time: 10 minutes

½ package (17.3 ounces) Pepperidge Farm® Frozen Puff Pastry Sheets (1 sheet)

½ cup prepared pesto sauce

½ cup drained, chopped oil-packed sun-dried tomatoes

THAW pastry sheet at room temperature 30 minutes. Preheat oven to 400°F.

UNFOLD pastry on lightly floured surface. Cut into 3 strips along fold marks. Cut each strip into 4 rectangles. Cut each rectangle diagonally to form triangles. Place triangles 1 inch apart on baking sheet. Bake for 15 minutes or until golden. Remove from baking sheet. Cool on wire rack.

SPLIT pastries into 2 layers, making 48 layers in all. Set aside **16** pastry top layers. Spread pesto evenly among **16** bottom pastry layers. Top with another pastry layer and tomatoes. Top with reserved pastry top layers.

Makes 16 Napoleons.

Sausage Bites

Thaw Time: 30 minutes
Prep Time: 20 minutes
Bake Time: 15 minutes

½ package (17.3 ounces) Pepperidge Farm® Frozen Puff Pastry Sheets (1 sheet)

½ pound bulk pork sausage*

THAW pastry sheet at room temperature 30 minutes. Preheat oven to 400°F.

UNFOLD pastry on lightly floured surface. Roll into 12×10-inch rectangle. Cut into 3 (3-inch) strips.

DIVIDE sausage into thirds. Roll each into a cylinder the length of the pastry. Place on edge of pastry strip. Starting at the long side, roll up. Press edges to seal.

CUT each roll into 12 (1-inch) slices. Place slices, cut-side down, 1½ inches apart, on 2 baking sheets. Bake 15 minutes or until golden and sausage is done. Serve warm.

Makes 36 appetizers.

*Substitute sweet **or** hot Italian pork sausage (casing removed) for bulk pork sausage.*

TIP:
To make pastries ahead, cut into slices and place on baking sheet. Freeze. When frozen, store in plastic bag for up to 1 month. To bake, preheat oven to 400°F. Place frozen slices on baking sheets. Bake 20 minutes or until golden and sausage is done.

Frosted Citrus Green Tea

Prep Time: 2 hours
Chill Time: 1 hour 30 minutes

4 cups (32 fluid ounces) Diet V8® Splash Tropical Blend Juice, chilled

4 cups strong brewed green tea

Fresh mint sprigs (optional)

Lemon slices (optional)

POUR **2 cups** juice into **1** ice cube tray. Freeze 1 hour 30 minutes or until frozen.

MIX remaining juice and tea and refrigerate at least 1 hour 30 minutes.

UNMOLD cubes and place 3 to 4 cubes in each of **6** glasses. Pour tea mixture into each glass. Serve with mint and lemon, if desired.

Makes about 8 cups.

Frosted Citrus Green Tea

Orange Mist

Prep Time: 5 minutes

1 can (46 fluid ounces) V8® 100% Vegetable Juice

1 can (6 ounces) frozen orange juice concentrate

1½ cups seltzer water **or** orange-flavored seltzer water

Ice cubes

MIX vegetable juice and orange juice. Add seltzer water. Serve over ice.

Makes 7 ½ cups.

Zesty Chicken Mozzarella Sandwiches

Prep Time: 10 minutes
Marinating Time: 10 minutes
Bake Time: 25 minutes

⅓ cup prepared Italian salad dressing

4 skinless, boneless chicken breast halves (about 1 pound)

1 loaf (11.75 ounces) Pepperidge Farm®Frozen Mozzarella Garlic Cheese Bread

1 medium red onion, sliced (about ½ cup)

POUR dressing in shallow nonmetallic dish. Add chicken and turn to coat. Cover and refrigerate 10 minutes.

PREHEAT oven to 400°F.

REMOVE bread from bag. Place frozen bread halves, cut-side up, on ungreased baking sheet. If bread halves are frozen together, carefully insert fork between halves to separate.

PLACE baking sheet on middle oven rack. Bake for 10 minutes or until heated through.

REMOVE chicken from marinade and place on lightly oiled grill rack over medium-hot coals. Grill uncovered 15 minutes or until chicken is no longer pink, turning and brushing often with dressing. Discard remaining dressing.

PLACE chicken and red onion on bottom bread half. Top with remaining bread half. Cut into quarters.

Makes 4 sandwiches.

Orange Mist

Barbecued Pork Spareribs
Recipe on page 26

Easy menus elegant enough to serve your guests

Perfect 4 Company

Just because a recipe is quick and simple doesn't mean it isn't special enough to serve company. It's not the complexity that makes a dish memorable, it's the combination of flavors. Likewise, the time it takes to prepare isn't important. What really matters is the love that was stirred in and the time spent sharing it at the table.

All the more reason to try one of these four wonderful company-class menus next time you plan a dinner party. The main dish, side dish, and dessert recipes for each meal all require no more than four ingredients! Yet the sum of the parts adds up to a fabulous meal fit for any guest.

Fast Friday Night with Friends

Menu 1

Vegetable Platter

Barbecued Pork Spareribs*

Coleslaw

Cheddar & Roasted Garlic Biscuits*

Lemonade

Easy Apple Strudel*

*recipe provided

TGIF Entertaining Tips

• Buy a ready-made vegetable platter from the supermarket produce section on your way home from work. Add a bowl of dip or salad dressing, and you have an instant appetizer.

• Set the table, make the lemonade, and prepare the grill before you leave in the morning. That way you'll have time to change out of your work clothes before everyone arrives.

• Go ahead and use good quality disposable partyware. There are wonderful colors and patterns available to brighten up your table. The prospect of easy clean-up can really brighten your mood, too!

Cheddar & Roasted Garlic Biscuits

Prep/Bake Time: 25 minutes

5 cups all-purpose baking **or** buttermilk biscuit mix

1 cup shredded Cheddar cheese (4 ounces)

1 can (14 ounces) Swanson® Seasoned Chicken Broth with Roasted Garlic

PREHEAT oven to 450°F.

MIX baking mix, cheese and broth to form a soft dough. Drop by spoonfuls onto 2 ungreased baking sheets, making 24.

BAKE for 10 minutes or until golden. Serve hot.

Makes 24 biscuits.

TIP:
Baked biscuits can be made ahead and frozen. To reheat, wrap loosely in aluminum foil. Heat in 375°F. oven for 10 minutes or until hot.

Barbecued Pork Spareribs

(pictured on page 22)

Prep Time: 15 minutes
Cook Time: 40 minutes

4 pounds pork spareribs

1 can (10¼ ounces) Campbell's® Beef Gravy

¾ cup barbecue sauce

2 tablespoons packed brown sugar

CUT ribs into serving pieces. Place ribs in saucepot. Cover with water. Heat to a boil. Cover and cook over low heat 30 minutes. Drain.

MIX gravy, barbecue sauce and brown sugar in large bowl. Add ribs. Toss gently to coat.

PLACE ribs on lightly oiled grill rack over medium-hot coals. Grill uncovered 10 minutes, turning once and brushing with gravy mixture occasionally.

Serves 4.

TIP:
Sauce may also be used for basting chicken.

Easy Apple Strudel

Thaw Time: 30 minutes
Prep Time: 10 minutes
Bake Time: 35 minutes

½ package (17.3 ounces) Pepperidge Farm® Frozen Puff Pastry Sheets (1 sheet)

1 egg

1 tablespoon water

1 can (21 ounces) apple pie filling

2 tablespoons raisins, optional

Confectioners' sugar, optional

THAW pastry sheet at room temperature 30 minutes. Preheat oven to 375°F. Mix egg and water.

UNFOLD pastry on lightly floured surface. Roll into 16×12-inch rectangle. With short side facing you, spoon pie filling on bottom half of pastry to within 1-inch of edges. sprinkle with raisins, if desired. Starting at short side, roll up like a jelly-roll. Place seam-side down on baking sheet. Tuck ends under to seal. Brush with egg mixture. Cut several 2-inch slits about 2 inches apart on top.

BAKE for 35 minutes or until golden. Cool on baking sheet on wire rack 30 minutes. Dust with confectioners' sugar, if desired; slice and serve warm.

Serves 6.

Easy Apple Strudel

Family Sunday Dinner

Menu 2

Roast Beef & Gravy*

Green Beans

Easy Caesar Salad*

Garlic Mashed Potatoes*

Iced Tea

Pear Mini-Turnovers*

*recipe provided

Make Family the Centerpiece

When the generations get together to share a meal, create a centerpiece that helps them share memories, too. Place a decorative tray, mirror, or cloth in the center of the table. Arrange several framed family photos—the older the better—on the tray. Add small vases of flowers, greenery, and votive candles for color. During dinner, ask one of the children to point out a photo of someone they don't recognize. Let one of the elders introduce the person in the photo and share some fun family stories about this interesting relative!

Easy Caesar Salad

Prep Time: 5 minutes

5 cups romaine lettuce torn in bite-size pieces (about 1 small head)

1 cup Pepperidge Farm® Generous Cut Classic Caesar Croutons

½ cup creamy Caesar salad dressing

Grated Parmesan cheese

TOSS lettuce, croutons and dressing in bowl until evenly coated. Top with cheese. Serve immediately.

Serves 4.

Garlic Mashed Potatoes

Prep/Cook Time: 25 minutes

2 cans (14 ounces **each**) Swanson® Seasoned Chicken Broth with Roasted Garlic

5 large potatoes, cut into 1-inch pieces (about 7½ cups)

Generous dash ground black pepper

PLACE broth and potatoes in medium saucepan over high heat. Heat to a boil. Cover and cook over medium heat 10 minutes or until potatoes are tender. Drain, reserving broth.

MASH potatoes with **1¼ cups** broth and black pepper. Add additional broth, if needed, until desired consistency.

Serves about 6.

Roast Beef & Gravy

Prep Time: 5 minutes
Cook Time: 1 hour 5 minutes

3½- to 4-pound boneless beef bottom round **or** chuck pot roast

1 can (14 ounces) Swanson® Beef **or** Lower Sodium Beef Broth (1¾ cups)

3 tablespoons all-purpose flour

PLACE roast in roasting pan. Roast at 350°F. for about 1 hour or until thermometer reads 155°F., basting frequently with some of the broth. Remove roast.

MIX 1 tablespoon drippings and flour in roasting pan. Gradually stir in remaining broth. Cook and stir until mixture boils and thickens. Slice roast and serve with gravy.

Serves 8.

Pear Mini-Turnovers

Thaw Time: 30 minutes
Prep Time: 15 minutes
Bake Time: 12 minutes

1 package (17.3 ounces) Pepperidge Farm® Frozen Puff Pastry Sheets (2 sheets)

2 small pears (about 8 ounces) peeled, cored and chopped

2 tablespoons raspberry preserves

Confectioners' sugar

THAW pastry sheets at room temperature for 30 minutes. Preheat oven to 400°F.

MIX pears and preserves.

UNFOLD pastry sheets on a lightly floured surface. Roll each sheet into 12-inch square and cut each into 12 rounds, using 3-inch cookie cutter. Spoon **1 rounded teaspoon** pear mixture into center of each square. Brush edges of squares with water and fold in half to form a half-moon. Press edges to seal. Place on baking sheets, about 2 inches apart.

BAKE for 12 minutes or until golden. Cool on wire rack 10 minutes. Sprinkle with confectioners' sugar.

Makes 24 pastries.

Book Club Dinner Meeting

Menu 3

Simply Delicious Meat Loaf & Gravy*

Garlic Seasoned Vegetables*

Potato Kabobs with Cheese Sauce*

Coffee and Tea

No Fuss Fruit Pie*

*recipe provided

4 Things to Do with Leftover Meat Loaf

Cold Sandwiches: Slice meat loaf thinly and serve on your favorite Pepperidge Farm® Bread with ketchup or barbecue sauce and pickle slices.

Square Meatballs: Cut meat loaf into cubes and add to your favorite Prego® pasta sauce before heating. Serve over hot cooked pasta.

Instant Hors d'oeuvres: Cut thin slices of meat loaf into squares and place atop your favorite Pepperidge Farm® crackers. Top with a dollop of horseradish sauce and a sprig of dill.

Quick Kabobs: Cut meat loaf into chunky cubes and alternate on wooden skewers with cubes of Cheddar cheese, grape tomatoes, and pimiento-stuffed olives. Add a small bowl of spicy ketchup for dipping.

Garlic Seasoned Vegetables

Prep/Cook Time: 20 minutes

1 can (14 ounces) Swanson® Seasoned Chicken Broth with Roasted Garlic

4 cups cut-up vegetables*

PLACE broth and vegetables in medium saucepan over high heat. Heat to a boil. Cover and cook over low heat 5 minutes or until vegetables are tender-crisp. Drain.

Serves 6.

Use any single vegetable or a combination, such as broccoli flowerets, cauliflower flowerets, sliced carrots and sliced celery.

TIP:
Recipe may be doubled.

Potato Kabobs with Cheese Sauce

Prep Time: 5 minutes
Cook Time: 30 minutes

6 medium baking potatoes (about 2 pounds)

2 tablespoons vegetable oil

1 can (10¾ ounces) Campbell's® Condensed Cheddar Cheese Soup

⅓ cup milk

CUT potatoes in half lengthwise. Cut each half crosswise into 4 pieces.

THREAD potatoes on **6** skewers. Brush with oil. Grill on lightly oiled grill rack over medium-hot coals 30 minutes or until tender, turning once.

MIX soup and milk in medium saucepan over medium-high heat. Heat through. Serve over potatoes.

Serves 6.

Simply Delicious Meat Loaf & Gravy

Prep Time: 5 minutes
Cook Time: 1 hour 5 minutes

1½ pounds ground beef

½ cup Italian-seasoned dry bread crumbs

1 egg, beaten

1 can (10¾ ounces) Campbell's® Condensed Golden Mushroom Soup

¼ cup water

MIX thoroughly beef, bread crumbs and egg. Shape **firmly** into 8×4-inch loaf in medium baking pan.

BAKE at 350°F. for 30 minutes. Spread **½ can** soup over top of meat loaf. Bake 30 minutes or until meat loaf is no longer pink.

MIX 2 tablespoons drippings, remaining soup and water in medium saucepan over medium heat. Heat through and serve with meat loaf.

Serves 6.

No-Fuss Fruit Pie

Thaw Time: 30 minutes
Prep Time: 10 minutes
Bake Time: 30 minutes

1 package (17.3 ounces) Pepperidge Farm® Frozen Puff Pastry Sheets (2 sheets)

1 egg

1 tablespoon water

1 can **or** jar (21 ounces) fruit pie filling

THAW pastry sheets at room temperature 30 minutes. Preheat oven to 400°F. Mix egg and water.

UNFOLD pastry sheets. Place **1** pastry sheet on baking sheet. Spread pie filling on pastry to within 1-inch of edges. Brush edges with egg mixture. Place remaining pastry sheet over pie filling. Press edges together with fork to seal. Brush with egg mixture. Cut several 2-inch slits in top of pastry.

BAKE for 30 minutes or until golden. Cool on baking sheet on wire rack at least 15 minutes. Cut into squares.

Serves 9.

Simply Delicious Meat Loaf & Gravy

Souper Bowl Party

Menu 4

Game-Winning Drumsticks*

Tossed Salad

Quick Bean & Rice Casserole*

Bread and Rolls

Splash & Rainbow Punch*

Tomato Soup Spice Cake*

*recipe provided

Score Points by Serving Buffet-Style

Make your party a buffet, so your guests don't miss out on any of the action. Remember these buffet basics:

• Place the buffet table away from the wall, if possible, so guests can help themselves from both sides.

• Give guests a helping hand. Put plates at the beginning of the buffet and finish with napkins, flatware, and drinks.

• Periodically check the food and replenish dishes as necessary. Make sure no serving utensils have been misplaced.

• For a fun football themed buffet, cover the table with a plastic green tablecloth divided into "yards" with white tape. Serve some foods from football helmets lined with foil. Identify what's in each dish with pennants cut from construction paper in the team colors and taped to wooden skewers. Cut napkins from inexpensive black and white striped cloth using pinking shears; roll them up and tie with twine. Add a plastic whistle to each one, if you dare!

Splash & Rainbow Punch

Prep Time: 5 minutes

½ cup chilled Diet V8 Splash® Juice, any flavor

½ cup chilled sparkling mineral water **or** seltzer water

Assorted sorbet (lime, raspberry, strawberry, peach, lemon **or** mango)

POUR juice and mineral water into tall glass. Add 5 mini scoops (⅓ cup) of various flavors of sorbet.

Serves 1.

TIP
Use a melon baller for scooping sorbet.

Quick Bean & Rice Casserole

Prep Time: 5 minutes
Cook Time: 25 minutes

2½ cups water

¾ cup **uncooked** regular long-grain white rice

1 pouch (2 ounces) Campbell's® Dry Onion Soup and Recipe Mix

1 can (15.75 ounces) Campbell's® Pork & Beans

¼ cup maple-flavored syrup

HEAT water to a boil in medium saucepan over high heat. Stir in rice and soup mix. Cover and cook over low heat 20 minutes or until rice is done and most of liquid is absorbed.

ADD beans and syrup. Heat through.

Serves 6.

Game-Winning Drumsticks

Prep Time: 10 minutes
Marinating Time: 4 hours
Bake Time: 1 hour

15 chicken drumsticks (about 4 pounds)

1 can (14 ounces) Swanson® Chicken **or** Natural Goodness™ Chicken Broth (1¾ cups)

½ cup Dijon-style mustard

⅓ cup Italian-seasoned dry bread crumbs

ARRANGE chicken in single layer in 15×10-inch disposable aluminum foil bakeware pan.

MIX broth and mustard. Pour broth mixture over chicken and turn to coat. Sprinkle bread crumbs over chicken. Cover and refrigerate 4 hours.

BAKE at 375°F. for 1 hour or until chicken is no longer pink.

SERVE immediately or let stand 30 minutes to serve at room temperature.

Serves about 6.

Tomato Soup Spice Cake

Prep Time: 10 minutes
Bake Time: 25 minutes

1 box (about 18 ounces) spice cake mix

1 can (10¾ ounces) Campbell's® Condensed Tomato Soup

½ cup water

2 eggs

PREHEAT oven to 350°F. Grease and lightly flour two 8-inch or 9-inch round cake pans.

MIX cake mix, soup, water and eggs according to package directions. Pour into prepared pans.

BAKE for 25 minutes or until toothpick inserted comes out clean.

COOL on wire racks 10 minutes. Remove from pans and cool completely.

FILL and frost with your favorite cream cheese frosting.

Serves 12.

Game-Winning Drumsticks

2-Step Chicken 'n' Biscuits
Recipe on page 42

Speedy, simple ways to put supper on the table

Weeknight Wonders

Some people are really organized—and then there's the rest of us! Monday through Friday at 5 p.m. most busy folks are not only wondering where the time went, but also "what's for dinner?"

This collection of simple recipes can answer that question in no time flat! Each quick meal idea combines classic, family-pleasing flavors with true, time-saving convenience: no more than four ingredients, easy techniques, and super-speedy preparation from start to finish. Now, even the most disorganized among us can get a home-cooked meal on the table every hectic, harried, and hurried night of the week!

2-Step Chicken 'n' Biscuits

(pictured on page 40)

Prep/Cook Time: 20 minutes

1 pound skinless, boneless chicken breasts, cut into cubes

1 can (10¾ ounces) Campbell's® Condensed Cream of Chicken **or** 98% Fat Free Cream of Chicken Soup

1 bag (16 ounces) frozen vegetable combination (broccoli, cauliflower, carrots)

8 hot biscuits, split

COOK chicken in medium nonstick skillet over medium-high heat until browned, stirring often.

ADD soup and vegetables. Cover and cook over low heat 5 minutes or until chicken is no longer pink. Serve on biscuits.

Serves 4.

Sirloin Steak Picante

Prep/Cook Time: 25 minutes

1½ pounds boneless beef sirloin **or** top round steak, 1½ inches thick

1 cup Pace® Picante Sauce **or** Chunky Salsa

PLACE steak on lightly oiled grill rack over medium-hot coals. Grill to desired doneness (allow 25 minutes for medium), turning once and brushing often with picante sauce. Thinly slice steak and serve with additional picante sauce.

Serves 6.

TIP:
To broil, place steak on rack in broiler pan. Broil 4 inches from heat to desired doneness (allow 25 minutes for medium), turning once and brushing often with picante sauce.

Sirloin Steak Picante

2-Step Italian Burger Melt

Prep/Bake Time: 25 minutes

6 ground beef patties

1 can (10¾ ounces) Campbell's® Condensed Tomato Soup

⅓ cup water

1 teaspoon dried oregano leaves, crushed

1 cup shredded mozzarella cheese (4 ounces)

PLACE patties in 2-quart shallow baking dish. Mix soup, water and oregano. Pour over patties. Top with cheese.

BAKE at 400°F. for 20 minutes or until patties are no longer pink. Serve on rolls or with pasta.

Serves 6.

2-Step Creamy Chicken & Pasta

Prep/Cook Time: 20 minutes

2 tablespoons vegetable oil

2 pounds skinless, boneless chicken breasts, cut into cubes

1 can (26 ounces) Campbell's® Condensed Cream of Chicken Soup

1 cup water

2 bags (16 ounces **each**) frozen vegetable and pasta blend

HEAT oil in saucepot over medium-high heat. Add chicken and cook until browned, stirring often.

ADD soup, water and vegetable pasta blend. Heat to a boil. Cover and cook over low heat 5 minutes or until pasta is done.

Serves 8.

2-Step Creamy Chicken & Pasta

Enchiladas

Prep Time: 15 minutes
Bake Time: 20 minutes

1 pound ground beef

1 jar (17.5 ounces) Pace® Enchilada Sauce

2 cups shredded cheese (8 ounces)

10 to 12 corn **or** flour tortillas (6-inch), warmed

PREHEAT oven to 350°F.

COOK beef in medium skillet over medium-high heat until beef is browned, stirring to separate meat. Pour off fat. Stir in **½ cup** sauce and **1 cup** cheese.

SPREAD ½ **cup** sauce in 3-quart shallow baking dish.

SPOON about 2 tablespoons beef mixture down center of each tortilla. Roll up and place seam-side down in baking dish. Top with remaining sauce and cheese.

BAKE for 20 minutes or until cheese is melted.

Makes 10 to 12 enchiladas.

French Onion Burgers

Prep/Cook Time: 20 minutes

1 pound ground beef

1 can (10½ ounces) Campbell's® Condensed French Onion Soup

4 slices cheese

4 round hard rolls, split

SHAPE beef into 4 patties, ½ inch thick.

COOK patties in medium skillet over medium heat 10 minutes or until no longer pink, turning once.

ADD soup. Heat to a boil. Cover and cook over low heat 5 minutes or until hot. Place cheese on patties and cook until cheese is melted.

SERVE on rolls with soup mixture for dipping.

Makes 4 burgers.

French Onion Burgers

Italiano Chicken & Rice

Prep Time: 5 minutes
Cook Time: 35 minutes

1 pound skinless, boneless chicken breasts, cut into strips

1 can (14 ounces) Swanson® Seasoned Chicken Broth with Italian Herbs

¾ cup **uncooked** regular long-grain white rice

¼ cup grated Parmesan cheese

COOK chicken in medium nonstick skillet over medium-high heat until browned, stirring often. Set chicken aside.

ADD broth and rice. Heat to a boil. Cover and cook over low heat 15 minutes.

STIR in cheese. Return chicken to pan. Cover and cook 5 minutes or until chicken is no longer pink and rice is done.

Serves 4.

2-Step Nacho Pasta

Prep/Cook Time: 20 minutes

4 cups **uncooked** corkscrew pasta

1 can (11 ounces) Campbell's® Condensed Fiesta Nacho Cheese Soup

½ cup milk

COOK pasta according to package directions. Drain.

MIX soup, milk and pasta in same saucepot over medium heat. Heat through.

Serves 4.

2-Step Nacho Pasta

Pasta Primavera

Prep/Cook Time: 25 minutes

3 cups **uncooked** corkscrew pasta

1 bag (16 ounces) frozen vegetable combination (broccoli, cauliflower, carrots)

1 jar (28 ounces) Prego® Traditional Pasta Sauce

Grated Parmesan cheese

COOK pasta according to package directions. Add vegetables for last 5 minutes of cooking time. Drain in colander.

HEAT pasta sauce in same saucepot over medium heat. Toss with pasta. Top with cheese.

Serves 4.

Tasty 2-Step Chicken

Prep/Cook Time: 20 minutes

1 tablespoon vegetable oil

4 skinless, boneless chicken breast halves (about 1 pound)

1 can (10¾ ounces) Campbell's® Condensed Cream of Mushroom **or** 98% Fat Free Cream of Mushroom Soup

½ cup water

HEAT oil in skillet over medium-high heat. Add chicken and cook 10 minutes or until browned. Set chicken aside. Pour off fat.

ADD soup and water. Heat to a boil. Return chicken to pan. Cover and cook over low heat 5 minutes or until chicken is no longer pink.

Serves 4.

Tasty 2-Step Chicken

2-Step Mushroom-Garlic Chicken

Prep/Cook Time: 20 minutes

1 tablespoon vegetable oil

4 skinless, boneless chicken breast halves (about 1 pound)

1 can (10¾ ounces) Campbell's® Condensed Cream of Mushroom with Roasted Garlic Soup

½ cup milk

HEAT oil in medium skillet over medium-high heat. Add chicken and cook 10 minutes or until browned.

ADD soup and milk. Heat to a boil. Cover and cook 5 minutes or until chicken is no longer pink.

Serves 4.

TIP:
Simmer fresh broccoli in Swanson® Chicken Broth for a delicious addition to your meal. For dessert, go à la mode—scoop vanilla ice cream over piping hot Pepperidge Farm® Peach Turnovers!

Tasty 2-Step Pork Chops

Prep/Cook Time: 20 minutes

1 tablespoon vegetable oil

4 pork chops, (about 1 pound), ½ inch thick

1 can (10¾ ounces) Campbell's® Condensed Cream of Mushroom **or** 98% Fat Free Cream of Mushroom Soup

½ cup water

HEAT oil in medium skillet over medium-high heat. Add chops and cook 10 minutes or until browned.

ADD soup and water. Heat to a boil. Cover and cook over low heat 5 minutes or until chops are no longer pink.

Serves 4.

TIP:
Serve with vegetable combination and mashed potatoes. For dessert serve chocolate pudding.

Tasty 2-Step Pork Chops

2-Step Herbed Chicken

Prep/Cook Time: 20 minutes

1 tablespoon vegetable oil

4 skinless, boneless chicken breast halves (about 1 pound)

1 can (10¾ ounces) Campbell's® Condensed Cream of Chicken with Herbs Soup

½ cup milk

HEAT oil in medium skillet over medium-high heat. Add chicken and cook 10 minutes or until browned.

ADD soup and milk. Heat to a boil. Cover and cook over low heat 5 minutes or until chicken is no longer pink.

Serves 4.

TIP:
Pair this dish with a colorful side of steamed snow peas and carrots. Have a Pepperidge Farm® Milano® milkshake for dessert: make a vanilla or chocolate milkshake and stir in crumbled Milano® cookies.

Grilled Beef Steak with Sautéed Onions

Prep Time: 5 minutes
Cook Time: 20 minutes

2 tablespoons olive oil

2 large onions, thinly sliced (about 2 cups)

2 pounds boneless beef sirloin, strip **or** rib steak, cut into 8 pieces

1 jar (16 ounces) Pace® Roasted Pepper & Garlic Salsa

HEAT **1 tablespoon** oil in medium skillet over medium heat. Add onions and cook until tender. Remove onions and keep warm.

HEAT remaining oil in same skillet. Add beef and cook until browned on both sides. Add salsa. Return onions to pan. Cook 3 minutes for medium-rare or until desired doneness.

Serves 8.

Grilled Beef Steak with Sautéed Onions

Souper Sloppy Joes

Prep/Cook Time: 15 minutes

1 pound ground beef

1 can (10¾ ounces) Campbell's® Condensed Tomato Soup

¼ cup water

1 tablespoon prepared yellow mustard

6 hamburger rolls, split

COOK beef in medium skillet over medium-high heat until beef is browned, stirring to separate meat. Pour off fat.

ADD soup, water and mustard. Heat through. Serve on rolls.

Serves 6.

Mushroom-Garlic Pork Chops

Prep/Cook Time: 20 minutes

1 tablespoon vegetable oil

4 pork chops, ½ inch thick (about 1 pound)

1 can (10¾ ounces) Campbell's® Condensed Cream of Mushroom with Roasted Garlic Soup

½ cup milk

HEAT oil in medium skillet over medium-high heat. Add chops and cook 10 minutes or until browned.

ADD soup and milk. Heat to a boil. Cover and cook over low heat 5 minutes or until chops are no longer pink.

Serves 4.

Mushroom-Garlic Pork Chops

2-Step Cheesy Pasta Twists

Prep/Cook Time: 20 minutes

6 cups cooked corkscrew pasta

1 jar (28 ounces) Prego® Traditional Pasta Sauce

1 cup shredded mozzarella cheese (4 ounces)

½ cup Pepperidge Farm® Zesty Italian Croutons, crushed

TOSS pasta with pasta sauce in medium skillet over medium heat. Heat through.

TOP with cheese and crushed croutons. Cover and cook over low heat until cheese is melted.

Serves 4.

Skillet Chicken Parmesan

Prep/Cook Time: 25 minutes
Stand Time: 5 minutes

6 tablespoons grated Parmesan cheese

1½ cups Prego® Traditional Pasta Sauce

6 small skinless, boneless chicken breast halves (about 1½ pounds)

1½ cups shredded part-skim mozzarella cheese (6 ounces)

STIR 4 tablespoons Parmesan cheese into pasta sauce.

SPRAY medium skillet with vegetable cooking spray and heat over medium-high heat 1 minute. Add chicken and cook 10 minutes or until browned. Drain.

POUR pasta sauce over chicken; turn chicken to coat both sides with sauce. Cover and cook over medium heat 10 minutes or until chicken is no longer pink.

TOP with mozzarella cheese and remaining Parmesan cheese. Let stand 5 minutes or until cheese is melted.

Serves 6.

Skillet Chicken Parmesan

Picante Chicken Quesadillas
Recipe on page 72

Kid Pleasers to Count On

Fun foods that are as simple as 1–2–3–4

Cooking for kids can be a challenge, but it also should be a fun and rewarding experience for everyone. Learn to make homemade foods that look good and taste great. Get your kids involved—the more they do, the better they'll eat and the prouder of their accomplishments they become. This chapter shares many easy-to-prepare simple recipes that apply the "4 ingredients or fewer" rule while incorporating tried-and-true kid favorites. Join your kids while together you whip up some tempting meals, satisfying snacks, easy treats, and a surprise or two.

Crispy Barbecue Chicken

Prep Time: 10 minutes
Bake Time: 1 hour

2 pounds chicken parts

½ cup barbecue sauce

2 cups Pepperidge Farm® Herb Seasoned Stuffing, crushed

DIP chicken into barbecue sauce. Coat with stuffing. Place chicken in shallow baking pan.

BAKE at 375°F. for 1 hour or until chicken is no longer pink.

Serves 4.

TIP:
For a savory corn muffin, use Swanson® Broth instead of milk when preparing your favorite corn muffin mix. Follow package directions, substituting an equal amount of broth for milk.

Cheese Fries

Prep/Bake Time: 20 minutes

1 bag (32 ounces) frozen French fried potatoes

1 can (10¾ ounces) Campbell's® Condensed Cheddar Cheese Soup

BAKE potatoes according to package directions.

PUSH potatoes into center of baking sheet. Stir soup in can and spoon over potatoes.

BAKE for 3 minutes or until soup is hot.

Serves 6.

Nacho Cheese Fries: Substitute Campbell's® Condensed Fiesta Nacho Cheese Soup for the Cheddar Cheese Soup.

Cheese Fries

Crunchy Ranch Chicken Nuggets

Prep/Bake Time: 25 minutes

1½ pounds skinless, boneless chicken breasts, cut into cubes

1 jar (12 ounces) refrigerated ranch salad dressing

2 cups Pepperidge Farm® Herb Seasoned Stuffing, crushed

DIP chicken into ¾ **cup** dressing. Coat with stuffing. Place chicken on baking sheet.

BAKE at 400°F. for 15 minutes or until chicken is no longer pink.

SERVE with remaining dressing for dipping.

Makes 40 appetizers.

TIP:
Dip grape tomatoes, celery sticks and zucchini in ranch style dressing for a crunchy, delicious side.

5-Minute Burrito Wraps

Prep/Cook Time: 5 minutes

1 can (11¼ ounces) Campbell's® Condensed Fiesta Chili Beef Soup

6 flour tortillas (8-inch)

Shredded Cheddar cheese

SPOON 2 tablespoons soup down center of each tortilla. Top with cheese. Fold sides over filling; fold up ends to enclose.

PLACE burritos seam-side down on microwavable plate. Microwave on **HIGH** 2 minutes or until hot.

Makes 6 burritos.

TIP:
Serve with extra Pace® Picante sauce and black beans.

5-Minute Burrito Wraps

Easy Potato Pancakes

Prep/Cook Time: 20 minutes

1 can (14 ounces) Swanson® Chicken **or** Natural Goodness™ Chicken Broth (1¾ cups)

Generous dash ground black pepper

1½ cups instant mashed potato flakes **or** buds

1 green onion, coarsely chopped

HEAT broth and black pepper to a boil in medium saucepan. Remove from heat. Add potato flakes and onion and stir until liquid is absorbed. Shape potato mixture into 4 (4-inch) pancakes.

COOK pancakes in medium nonstick skillet over medium heat until browned on both sides.

Serves 4.

TIP:
Layer your choice of fruit and yogurt to make a delicious parfait for dessert.

Cheeseburger Pasta

Prep/Cook Time: 20 minutes

1 pound ground beef

1 can (10¾ ounces) Campbell's® Condensed Cheddar Cheese Soup

1 can (10¾ ounces) Campbell's® Condensed Tomato Soup

1½ cups water

2 cups **uncooked** medium shell pasta

COOK beef in medium skillet over medium-high heat until beef is browned, stirring to separate meat. Pour off fat.

ADD soups, water and pasta. Heat to a boil. Cook over medium heat 10 minutes or until pasta is done, stirring often.

Serves 4.

TIP:
Serve a hearty salad of tomatoes and fresh mozzarella cheese tossed with basil, olive oil and balsamic vinegar.

Cheeseburger Pasta

Franks Under Wraps

Thaw Time: 30 minutes
Prep Time: 15 minutes
Bake Time: 15 minutes

½ package (17.3 ounces) Pepperidge Farm® Frozen Puff Pastry Sheets (1 sheet)

1 egg

1 tablespoon water

10 frankfurters (about 1 pound), cut crosswise into halves

Prepared mustard

THAW pastry sheet at room temperature 30 minutes. Preheat oven to 400°F. Mix egg and water.

UNFOLD pastry on lightly floured surface. Cut into 20 (½-inch) strips. Wrap pastry strips around frankfurters, pressing gently to seal. Place 2 inches apart on baking sheet. Brush with egg mixture.

BAKE for 15 minutes or until golden. Serve with mustard for dipping.

Makes 20 appetizers.

Sloppy Joe Pizza

Prep/Bake Time: 20 minutes

¾ pound ground beef

1 can (10¾ ounces) Campbell's® Condensed Tomato Soup

1 Italian bread shell (12-inch)

1½ cups shredded Cheddar cheese (6 ounces)

PREHEAT oven to 450°F.

COOK beef in medium skillet over medium-high heat until beef is browned, stirring to separate meat. Pour off fat.

ADD soup and heat through. Spread beef mixture over shell to within ¼ inch of edge. Top with cheese. Bake for 12 minutes or until cheese is melted.

Serves 4.

Sloppy Joe Pizza

Power Breakfast Sandwiches

Prep Time: 5 minutes

¼ cup peanut butter

4 slices Pepperidge Farm® 100% Stoneground Whole Wheat Natural Whole Grain Bread

¼ cup raisins*

1 medium banana, sliced*

SPREAD peanut butter on **4** bread slices. Divide raisins and banana between **2** bread slices. Top with remaining bread slices, peanut butter-side down. Cut in half.

Makes 2 sandwiches.

Substitute 1 large apple, cored and sliced, for raisins and banana.

Easy Beef & Pasta

Prep/Cook Time: 20 minutes

1 pound boneless beef sirloin **or** top round steak, ¾ inch thick

1 tablespoon vegetable oil

1 can (10¾ ounces) Campbell's® Condensed Tomato Soup

½ cup water

1 bag (about 16 ounces) frozen vegetable and pasta blend

SLICE beef into very thin strips.

HEAT oil in medium skillet over medium-high heat. Add beef and cook until browned, stirring often.

ADD soup, water and vegetable pasta blend. Heat to a boil. Cover and cook over low heat 5 minutes or until pasta is done.

Serves 4.

Easy Beef & Pasta

Picante Chicken Quesadillas

(pictured on page 60)

Prep Time: 10 minutes
Bake Time: 5 minutes

1 can (10¾ ounces) Campbell's®
  Condensed Cheddar Cheese
  Soup

¼ cup Pace® Picante Sauce

1½ cups chopped cooked chicken

8 flour tortillas (8-inch), warmed

PREHEAT oven to 425°F.

MIX soup, picante sauce and chicken.

PLACE tortillas on **2** baking sheets. Top half of each tortilla with **¼ cup** soup mixture. Spread to within ½ inch of edge. Moisten edges of tortilla with water. Fold over and press edges together.

BAKE for 5 minutes or until hot.

Makes 8 quesadillas.

Frosty Fruit Cooler

Prep Time: 10 minutes

1 cup V8® Splash Orange
  Pineapple Juice

½ cup cut-up strawberries **or**
  raspberries

½ cup ice cubes

¼ cup vanilla yogurt

PLACE juice, strawberries, ice cubes and yogurt in blender. Cover and blend until smooth.

Makes 2 cups.

TIP:
Pour into an insulated thermos so kids can take it with them on-the-go.

Frosty Fruit Cooler

Peanut Butter Banana "Tacos"

Prep Time: 10 minutes

4 tablespoons crunchy peanut butter*

4 slices Pepperidge Farm® Cinnamon Swirl **or** Raisin Cinnamon Swirl Bread

1 medium ripe banana

SPREAD peanut butter among bread slices.

CUT banana into crosswise halves. Cut each half into 2 lengthwise pieces. Place banana piece on each prepared bread slice and roll up.

Serves 4.

Substitute cream cheese or jelly for the peanut butter.

Mozzarella Meatball Sandwiches

Prep Time: 5 minutes
Bake Time: 10 minutes
Cook Time: 20 minutes

1 loaf (11.75 ounces) Pepperidge Farm® Frozen Mozzarella & Garlic Cheese Bread

½ cup Prego® Traditional Pasta Sauce

12 (½ ounce **each**) **or** 6 (1 ounce **each**) frozen meatballs

PREHEAT oven to 400°F.

REMOVE bread from bag. Place frozen bread halves, cut-side up, on ungreased baking sheet. If bread halves are frozen together, carefully insert fork between halves to separate.

PLACE baking sheet on middle oven rack. Bake for 10 minutes or until heated through.

PLACE pasta sauce and meatballs in medium saucepan. Cook over medium heat 20 minutes or until heated through.

PLACE meatballs onto bottom bread half. Top with remaining bread half. Cut into quarters.

Makes 4 sandwiches.

Mozzarella Meatball Sandwiches

Goldfish® Haystacks

Prep Time: 15 minutes

1 package (10 ounces) peanut butter chips

1 tablespoon vegetable shortening

1 cup chow mein noodles

1 cup Pepperidge Farm® Goldfish® Colors Baked Snack Crackers

LINE baking sheet with waxed paper.

PLACE chips and shortening in microwavable plate. Microwave on **HIGH** (100% power) 1 minute. Stir until smooth. Microwave 15 seconds if needed.

ADD noodles and crackers and stir to coat.

DROP mixture by tablespoons onto prepared baking sheet. Top each with an additional cracker. Let stand until firm. If necessary, cover and refrigerate until firm. Cover and store in tightly covered container.

Makes 24.

TIP:
Use your favorite flavor chips or use ¾ **cup** Pepperidge Farm® Goldfish® Colors and ¼ **cup** flaked coconut

Fishy Families

Prep Time: 5 minutes
Cook Time: 1 minute 15 seconds
Chill Time: 30 minutes

1 package (12 ounces) semi-sweet chocolate pieces (2 cups)

2½ cups Pepperidge Farm® Pretzel Goldfish® Baked Snack Crackers

1 container (4 ounces) multi-colored nonpareils

PLACE chocolate in microwavable bowl. Microwave on **HIGH** 1 minute. Stir. Microwave at 15 second intervals, stirring after each, until chocolate is melted. Stir in crackers to coat.

SCOOP cracker mixture with a tablespoon and drop onto waxed paper-lined baking sheet. Sprinkle with nonpareils. Repeat with remaining cracker mixture and nonpareils.

REFRIGERATE 30 minutes or until firm. Store in refrigerator.

Makes 1 pound.

Jump Start Smoothie

Prep Time: 10 minutes

2 cups V8 Splash® Orange
   Pineapple Juice, chilled

1 cup low-fat vanilla yogurt

2 cups frozen whole strawberries
   or raspberries

PLACE juice, yogurt and
strawberries in blender or food
processor. Cover and blend until
smooth.

Makes about 4 cups.

Jump Start Smoothie

Souper Nachos

Prep Time: 5 minutes
Cook Time: 3 minutes

1 can (10¾ ounces) Campbell's®
   Condensed Cheddar Cheese
   Soup

½ cup Pace® Picante Sauce

   Tortilla chips

MIX soup and picante sauce in
microwavable bowl. Microwave
on **HIGH** 3 minutes or until hot.

SERVE with chips for dipping **or**
pour over chips.

Makes 1¾ cups.

Splash Ice Cream Soda

Prep Time: 5 minutes

½ cup chilled V8® Splash Juice,
   any flavor

½ cup chilled seltzer **or** lemon-
   lime soda

¼ cup vanilla ice cream

POUR juice and seltzer into glass.
Top with ice cream.

Makes about 1 cup.

Broth Simmered Rice
Recipe on page 80

Side Dish
Fast and flavorful recipes to round out the meal
Shortcuts

Almost any entrée seems special when it's accompanied by delicious side dishes. Monday night meat loaf becomes a "blue plate special" beside fluffy mashed potatoes and glazed carrots. A rotisserie chicken from the market tastes like Sunday dinner when it's paired with stuffing. Easy tacos are especially good complemented with spiced up Mexican-style rice. Yet we often don't have time—or at least we *think* we don't have time—to make interesting and appealing side dishes part of the weekday menu.

These side dish shortcuts are not only long on flavor, they're also some of the easiest dishes to put on the table. They include wonderful ideas that can double as vegetarian entrées and some deceptively simple sides that will even impress your guests.

Broth Simmered Rice

(pictured on page 78)

Prep/Cook Time: 25 minutes

1 can (14 ounces) Swanson® Chicken **or** Natural Goodness™ Chicken Broth (1¾ cups)*

¾ cup **uncooked** regular long-grain white rice

HEAT broth to a boil in medium saucepan over high heat. Stir in rice. Cover and cook over low heat 20 minutes or until rice is done.

Serves 4.

*Substitute Swanson® Beef, Vegetable **or** Seasoned Broths for the Chicken Broth.*

Cheesy Broccoli

Prep/Cook Time: 10 minutes

1 can (10¾ ounces) Campbell's® Condensed Cheddar Cheese Soup

¼ cup milk

4 cups frozen broccoli cuts

MIX soup and milk in 2-quart microwavable casserole. Add broccoli. **Cover.**

MICROWAVE on **HIGH** 8 minutes or until broccoli is tender-crisp, stirring once.

Serves 4.

Cheesy Broccoli

Souper Quick Gumbo Rice

Prep Time: 5 minutes
Cook Time: 5 minutes
Stand Time: 5 minutes

1 can (10¾ ounces) Campbell's® Condensed Chicken Gumbo Soup

1 cup water

⅛ teaspoon garlic powder

⅛ teaspoon onion powder

1¼ cups **uncooked** instant white rice

HEAT soup, water, garlic powder and onion powder in medium saucepan over medium-high heat to a boil.

STIR in rice. Cover and remove from heat. Let stand 5 minutes. Fluff with fork.

Serves 3.

Creamy Vegetables in Pastry Shells

Bake Time: 30 minutes
Prep/Cook Time: 15 minutes

1 package (10 ounces) Pepperidge Farm® Frozen Puff Pastry Shells

1 can (10¾ ounces) Campbell's® Condensed Cream of Mushroom **or** 98% Fat Free Cream of Mushroom Soup

⅓ cup milk **or** water

1 bag (16 ounces) frozen vegetable combination (broccoli, cauliflower, carrots), cooked and drained

BAKE pastry shells according to package directions.

MIX soup and milk in medium saucepan over medium heat. Heat through. Divide vegetables among pastry shells. Spoon sauce over vegetables and pastry shells.

Serves 6.

Creamy Vegetables in Pastry Shells

Saucy Asparagus

Prep/Cook Time: 10 minutes

1 can (10¾ ounces) Campbell's®
   Condensed Cream of
   Asparagus Soup

⅓ cup milk

2 pounds asparagus, trimmed **or**
   2 packages (about 10 ounces
   each) frozen asparagus spears,
   cooked and drained

MIX soup and milk in medium
saucepan over medium heat. Heat
through. Serve over asparagus.

Serves 6.

Fiesta Tomato Rice

Prep Time: 5 minutes
Cook Time: 5 minutes
Stand Time: 5 minutes

1 can (10½ ounces) Campbell's®
   Condensed Chicken Broth

½ cup water

½ cup Pace® Thick & Chunky
   Salsa

2 cups **uncooked** instant white
   rice

MIX broth, water and salsa in
medium saucepan over medium-
high heat. Heat to a boil.

STIR in rice. Cover and remove
from heat. Let stand 5 minutes.
Fluff with fork.

Serves 4.

Onion Bean Bake

Prep Time: 10 minutes
Bake Time: 1 hour

2 cans (28 ounces **each**)
   Campbell's® Pork & Beans

1 pouch (2 ounces) Campbell's®
   Dry Onion Soup and Recipe
   Mix

2 tablespoons maple-flavored
   syrup

4 slices bacon, cut in half and
   partially cooked

MIX beans, soup mix and syrup in
2-quart shallow baking dish. Top
with bacon.

BAKE at 350°F. for 1 hour or until
hot.

Serves 11.

Creamy Souper Rice

Prep/Cook Time: 20 minutes
Stand Time: 15 minutes

1 can (10¾ ounces) your favorite
   Campbell's® Condensed
   Cream Soup

1 soup can water

1 soup can **uncooked** instant
   white rice

HEAT soup and water to a boil in
medium saucepan over high heat.

STIR in rice. Cover and remove from
heat. Let stand 15 minutes or until
rice is done.

Serves 4.

Souper Quick Southwestern Rice and Beans

Prep Time: 5 minutes
Cook Time: 5 minutes
Stand Time: 5 minutes

1 can (10¾ ounces) Campbell's® Condensed Southwestern-Style Chicken Vegetable Soup

1 cup water

1¼ cups **uncooked** instant white rice

HEAT soup and water to a boil in medium saucepan over medium-high heat.

STIR in rice. Cover and remove from heat. Let stand 5 minutes. Fluff with fork.

Serves 3.

Savory Vegetables

Prep/Cook Time: 20 minutes

1 cup Swanson® Chicken **or** Natural Goodness™ Chicken Broth

3 cups cut-up vegetables*

MIX broth and vegetables in medium saucepan over high heat. Heat to a boil.

COVER and cook over low heat 5 minutes or until vegetables are tender-crisp. Drain.

Serves 4.

*Use any combination of vegetables you like, including broccoli flowerets, cauliflower flowerets, sliced carrots, bell pepper strips, onion wedges, snow peas, and sliced celery.

Savory Vegetables

Fiesta Potatoes

Prep/Cook Time: 25 minutes

1 can (10¾ ounces) Campbell's® Condensed Cheddar Cheese Soup

½ cup Pace® Chunky Salsa

¼ cup milk

5 medium potatoes (about 1¼ pounds), cooked and sliced ¼-inch thick

MIX soup, salsa and milk in medium skillet over medium heat. Add potatoes. Heat through.

Serves 5.

Skinny Mashed Sweet Potatoes

Prep/Cook Time: 25 minutes

2 cans (14 ounces **each**) Swanson® Chicken **or** Natural Goodness™ Chicken Broth (3½ cups)

4 large sweet potatoes **or** yams, cut into 1-inch pieces (about 7½ cups)

Generous dash ground black pepper

2 tablespoons packed brown sugar

PLACE broth and potatoes in medium saucepan over high heat. Heat to a boil. Cover and cook over medium heat 10 minutes or until potatoes are tender. Drain, reserving broth.

MASH potatoes with **1¼ cups** broth and black pepper. Add additional broth, if needed, until desired consistency. Add brown sugar.

Serves 6.

Skinny Mashed Sweet Potatoes

Mushroom-Garlic Oven Baked Risotto

Prep Time: 5 minutes
Bake Time: 45 minutes

1 can (10¾ ounces) Campbell's® Condensed Cream of Mushroom with Roasted Garlic Soup

3⅓ cups water

½ teaspoon dried thyme leaves, crushed

1¼ cups **uncooked** regular long-grain white rice

¼ cup slivered almonds

MIX soup, water, thyme, rice and almonds in 2-quart casserole. **Cover.**

BAKE at 375°F. for 45 minutes or until rice is done. Stir. (Risotto will absorb liquid as it stands.)

Serves 4.

Fruited Chunky Salsa

Prep Time: 10 minutes
Marinating Time: 15 minutes

1 jar (12 ounces) Pace® Chunky Salsa, any variety

2 tablespoons chopped fresh cilantro leaves

1 teaspoon lime juice

1 mango, diced (about 1 cup)

MIX salsa, cilantro, lime juice and mango. Let stand 15 minutes. Serve as a condiment for pork, poultry or seafood.

Makes 2¾ cups.

Garden Vegetable Stuffing

Prep Time: 10 minutes
Bake Time: 20 minutes

1 can (14 ounces) Swanson® Chicken **or** Natural Goodness™ Chicken Broth (1¾ cups)

3 cups cut-up vegetables*

5 cups Pepperidge Farm® Cubed Herb Seasoned Stuffing

PLACE broth and vegetables in medium saucepan over high heat. Heat to a boil. Cover and cook over low heat 5 minutes or until vegetables are tender-crisp. Remove from heat.

ADD stuffing. Mix lightly. Spoon into greased 1½-quart casserole.

BAKE at 350°F. for 20 minutes or until hot.

Serves 8.

Use a combination of broccoli flowerets, cauliflower flowerets, sliced carrots and sliced celery.

Italian Herb Seasoned Vegetables

Prep/Cook Time: 20 minutes

1 can (14 ounces) Swanson® Seasoned Chicken Broth with Italian Herbs

½ teaspoon garlic powder

4 cups cut-up vegetables*

1 tablespoon grated Parmesan cheese

PLACE broth, garlic powder and vegetables in medium saucepan over high heat. Heat to a boil. Cover and cook over low heat 5 minutes or until tender-crisp. Drain. Sprinkle with cheese.

Serves 4.

Use a combination of broccoli flowerets, cauliflower flowerets, sliced carrots and sliced celery.

Index

Index

METRIC CONVERSION CHART

VOLUME MEASUREMENTS (dry)

⅛ teaspoon = 0.5 mL
¼ teaspoon = 1 mL
½ teaspoon = 2 mL
¾ teaspoon = 4 mL
1 teaspoon = 5 mL
1 tablespoon = 15 mL
2 tablespoons = 30 mL
¼ cup = 60 mL
⅓ cup = 75 mL
½ cup = 125 mL
⅔ cup = 150 mL
¾ cup = 175 mL
1 cup = 250 mL
2 cups = 1 pint = 500 mL
3 cups = 750 mL
4 cups = 1 quart = 1 L

VOLUME MEASUREMENTS (fluid)

1 fluid ounce (2 tablespoons) = 30 mL
4 fluid ounces (½ cup) = 125 mL
8 fluid ounces (1 cup) = 250 mL
12 fluid ounces (1½ cups) = 375 mL
16 fluid ounces (2 cups) = 500 mL

WEIGHTS (mass)

½ ounce = 15 g
1 ounce = 30 g
3 ounces = 90 g
4 ounces = 120 g
8 ounces = 225 g
10 ounces = 285 g
12 ounces = 360 g
16 ounces = 1 pound = 450 g

DIMENSIONS

1/16 inch = 2 mm
⅛ inch = 3 mm
¼ inch = 6 mm
½ inch = 1.5 cm
¾ inch = 2 cm
1 inch = 2.5 cm

OVEN TEMPERATURES

250°F = 120°C
275°F = 140°C
300°F = 150°C
325°F = 160°C
350°F = 180°C
375°F = 190°C
400°F = 200°C
425°F = 220°C
450°F = 230°C

BAKING PAN SIZES

Utensil	Size in Inches/Quarts	Metric Volume	Size in Centimeters
Baking or Cake Pan (square or rectangular)	8×8×2	2 L	20×20×5
	9×9×2	2.5 L	23×23×5
	12×8×2	3 L	30×20×5
	13×9×2	3.5 L	33×23×5
Loaf Pan	8×4×3	1.5 L	20×10×7
	9×5×3	2 L	23×13×7
Round Layer Cake Pan	8×1½	1.2 L	20×4
	9×1½	1.5 L	23×4
Pie Plate	8×1¼	750 mL	20×3
	9×1¼	1 L	23×3
Baking Dish or Casserole	1 quart	1 L	—
	1½ quart	1.5 L	—
	2 quart	2 L	—

Notes